Contents

preteen Bible study series

Building Friendships

Loveland, Colorado

Group's R.E.A.L. Guarantee® to you:

This Group resource incorporates our R.E.A.L. approach to ministry—one that encourages long-term retention and life transformation. It's ministry that's:

Relational
Because learner-to-learner interaction enhances learning and builds Christian friendships.

Experiential
Because what learners experience through discussion and action sticks with them up to 9 times longer than what they simply hear or read.

Applicable
Because the aim of Christian education is to equip learners to be both hearers and doers of God's Word.

Learner-based
Because learners understand and retain more when the learning process takes into consideration how they learn best.

preteen Bible study series

Building Friendships

Copyright © 2004 Group Publishing, Inc.

Visit our Web site: **www.grouppublishing.com**

Credits
Authors: Linda Snyder, Steve and Annie Wamburg
Editor: Jim Hawley
Creative Development Editor: Karl Leuthauser
Chief Creative Officer: Joani Schultz
Copy Editor: Linda Marcinkowski
Art Director: Kari K. Monson
Cover Art Director/Designer: Jeff Spencer
Cover Photographer: Daniel Treat
Print Production Artist: Tracy K. Hindman
Illustrator: Shawn Banner
Production Manager: DeAnne Lear

Unless otherwise noted, Scripture taken from the HOLY BIBLE, NEW INTERNATIONAL VERSION®. Copyright © 1973, 1978, 1984 by International Bible Society. Used by permission of Zondervan Publishing House. All rights reserved.

ISBN 0-7644-2493-9
10 9 8 7 6 5 4 3 2 1   13 12 11 10 09 08 07 06 05 04
Printed in the United States of America.

Introduction:
Building Friendships

Preteens are entering a reality where friendships are becoming increasingly important. And they have a lot of choices concerning the friendships they'll form. *Building Friendships* will help preteens discover how God can help them to be faithful friends, displaying Christlike qualities as they interact with their peers. In the first study, they'll explore quality friendships that can withstand the pressure to compromise. They will discover ways God can help them to develop friendship qualities that will build strong friendships.

> Preteens are entering a reality where friendships are becoming increasingly important.

Next, preteens will explore what to do when conflicts arise. They will look at how important honesty is in a friendship, and discover ways God can help them resolve conflict and restore trust in friendships.

In the third study, your students will explore how to relate to the opposite sex. They will look at how God values men and women equally, and they'll learn the importance of displaying Christian maturity as they relate to the opposite sex.

In any friendship, human failure will be evident. As preteens face letting down or being let down by a friend, they may get discouraged. The last study will help them see how Jesus is a friend who will never let them down. As important as earthly friendships become to preteens, a relationship with Jesus is the best friendship they could ever have!

About Faith 4 Life™: Preteen Bible Study Series

The Faith 4 Life™: Preteen Bible Study Series helps preteens take a Bible-based approach to faith and life issues. Each book in the series contains these important elements:

- **Life application of Bible truth**—Faith 4 Life studies help preteens understand what the Bible says, and then apply that truth to their lives.

- **A relevant topic**—Each Faith 4 Life book focuses on one main topic, with four studies to give your students a thorough understanding of how the Bible relates to that topic.

- **One point**—Each study makes one point, centering on that one theme to make sure students really understand the important truth it conveys. This point is stated upfront and throughout the study.

- **Simplicity**—The studies are easy to use. Each contains a "Before the Study" box that outlines any advance preparation required. Each study also contains a "Study at a Glance" chart so you can quickly and easily see what supplies you'll need and what each study will involve.

- **Action and interaction**—Each study relies on experiential learning to help students learn what God's Word has to say. Preteens discuss and debrief their experiences in large groups, small groups, and individual reflection.

- **Reproducible handouts**—Faith 4 Life books include reproducible handouts for students. No need for student books!

- **Flexible options**—Faith 4 Life preteen studies have two opening and two closing activities. You can choose the options that work best for your students, time frame, or supply needs.

- **Follow-up ideas**—At the end of each book, you'll find a section called "Changed 4 Life." This provides ideas for following up with your students to make sure the Bible truths stick with them.

Use Faith 4 Life studies to show your preteens how the Bible is relevant to their lives. Help them see that God can invade every area of their lives and change them in ways they can only imagine. Encourage your students to go deeper into faith—faith that will sustain them for life! Faith 4 Life, forever!

What Makes a Friend?

The Point: ➤ God can help us develop good friendships.

As children become preteens, the importance of having friends becomes stronger. And that may mean having the "right" friends. But kids may do unwise things to become friends with a popular person. They need the skills to evaluate their relationships as they look for healthy friendships. By helping preteens recognize the Christian qualities good friends should have, we can help them build strong, healthy relationships. Use this study to help preteens understand how God can help them develop healthy friendships.

Scripture Source

1 Samuel 20:1-42

This passage tells the story of David and Jonathan's friendship against the backdrop of King Saul's treachery. When David and Jonathan met, they struck up an almost instant friendship. But Saul's jealousy of David was so great that Saul tried to kill David. Jonathan had to choose between his father's wishes and his love for David. Jonathan chose to be true to David, and protected him from Saul, even though the cost was high.

Proverbs 17:17

Proverbs 17:17 describes the qualities of a true friend. Solomon wrote much of the book of Proverbs as a collection of little bits of wisdom he'd picked up over the years. This particular verse gives us a picture of a real friend, one who's always there when you need him or her, and one who loves you—no matter what.

Matthew 11:18-19

The passage speaks of the people's perceptions of Jesus and John the Baptist during their ministries on earth. In this passage, Jesus confronts the people for basing their opinions of others on the company they keep. Jesus wasn't afraid to be friends with the less popular people of his day, no matter what others might have said about him.

John 15:13

In John 15:13, Jesus describes the ultimate act of friendship. During the Last Supper, the Passover meal before Jesus' death, Jesus spoke about love and told his disciples that the ultimate sign of love and friendship is to die for a friend.

The Study at a Glance

Section	Minutes	What Students Will Do	Supplies
Warm-Up Option 1	up to 10	**Friendship Factors**—Brainstorm qualities that make some-one a good friend.	Paper, pens, newsprint, markers, tape
Warm-Up Option 2	up to 10	**Act Like a Friend**—Pantomime friendly actions.	
Bible Connection	up to 20	**A Special Friendship**—Perform a skit of David and Jonathan's friendship and explore 1 Samuel 20.	Bibles, "The Friendship Show" handouts (pp. 14-15), newsprint, markers
	up to 15	**Quality Check**—Consider biblical advice as they rate their own friendship qualities.	Bibles, "Quality Check" handouts (p. 16), pens
Life Application	up to 10	**Friendship Improvement**—Choose one friendship quality to improve on this week and create a symbol of that quality.	A variety of art supplies
Wrap Up Option1	up to 10	**Friendship Collage**—Create a collage that illustrates friendship.	Old magazines, several rolls of tape, newsprint
Wrap-Up Option 2	up to 10	**Friendsong**—Listen to and discuss a popular song about friendship.	CD with current popular song about friendship, CD player

Before the Study

Set out Bibles, paper, pens, newsprint, markers, tape, CD of a current popular song about friendship, CD player, old magazines, and art supplies such as clay, paint, and poster board. Make one photocopy of the "Quality Check" handout (p. 16) for each preteen. Also make enough photocopies of the "Friendship Show" script (pp. 14-15) for all the speaking roles.

The Study

Friendship Factors *(up to 10 minutes)*

Form groups of up to four. Give each group a piece of paper and a pen. Instruct groups to come up with as many character traits or actions as possible that build good friendships. Give preteens a few minutes to create their lists. Then have a member from each group display the group's list. Have group members compare the posted lists and then create a composite list on newsprint with markers. Tape the composite list to the wall.

Say: **You've created a list of character traits and actions that friends possess. Ask:**

- **What surprised you about our list?**

- **Is it easy or hard to possess these qualities?**

Have preteens answer the next question silently. **Ask:**

- **Based on these qualities, do you think you would say you are a good friend?**

Say: **We all need friends. And I think it's safe to say we want to be good friends as well. Today we're beginning a study series about friendships. We're going to look at how ►God can help us develop good friendships. Let's get started.**

◄ *The Point*

Warm-Up Option 2

Act Like a Friend *(up to 10 minutes)*

Have preteens form pairs. **Say:** **I want you to think about these next few questions without answering aloud. Ask:**

- **What makes a good friend?**

- **What things do they do that show they are good friends?**

- **What qualities do they have?**

Say: **Now I want you and your partner to come up with a simple mime that shows an answer to one of the questions I asked.**

Allow students a few minutes to prepare their mimes. Then have pairs perform their mimes, and encourage preteens to guess the characteristic. After each pair has had a turn, have students gather in a circle. **Ask:**

- **Was it easy or hard to mime "friend characteristics"?**
- **Is it easy or hard showing these characteristics toward your friends in real life?**

Say: It may not be easy to be a good friend sometimes. It's one thing to know what to do and another to do it. But the good news is that God can help us with both areas. Today we're beginning a study series about friendships.

The Point ➤ We're going to look at how ➤God can help us develop good friendships. Let's get started.

FYI

If you have fewer than nine students, combine the audience members' speaking roles.

FYI

To make the show more realistic, you might want to dress the three Bible characters in simple period clothing, such as a sheet draped over each person and a towel for a headdress. You also could use microphones with a karaoke machine for the announcer, host, and audience members with speaking parts.

Bible Connection

A Special Friendship *(up to 20 minutes)*

Give each assigned speaker a photocopy of the "Friendship Show" handout (pp. 14-15). Assign the following roles: Announcer, Host, David, Jonathan, King Saul, and Audience Members 1 to 4. Have remaining kids form the general audience. Set up three chairs at the front of your room and have David, Jonathan, and Saul sit down. Place the four audience members with speaking roles in the general audience area, facing the three Bible characters. Have the announcer begin the show by reading his or her opening part. Have kids read their show parts. After the show is finished, have cast members join the audience group.

Ask:

- **What qualities did you see in David and Jonathan's friendship?**
- **How did their commitment to God affect their friendship?**

Say: Our friendship show gave us an idea of the hard times David and Jonathan faced. Let's explore the actual Bible story to give us a better idea of how special their friendship was.

Form five groups and assign the following 1 Samuel 20 passages to individual groups: verses 1-9, verses 10-17, verses 18-27, verses 28-34, and verses 35-42. Provide Bibles, newsprint, and markers to groups. Have group members work together and write an approximately three-sentence summary of the part of David and Jonathan's story their group was assigned. Allow a few minutes for groups to create their summaries. Then have groups present their newsprint summaries in story order. After the story has been summarized, have groups discuss the following questions within their groups. **Ask:**

• How hard would it be for you if you had been in David and Jonathan's situation? Explain.

• How were David and Jonathan loyal to each other?

• How important is loyalty in a friendship? Why?

• How were David and Jonathan honest with each other?

• How important is honesty in a friendship? Why?

After groups have discussed the questions, **say: Seeing the importance of loyalty and honesty in a friendship is a way that ➤God can help us develop good friendships. Let's look at some other friendship qualities God's Word shows us.**

F9I

Whenever groups discuss a list of questions, write the questions on newsprint, and tape the newsprint to the wall so groups can discuss the questions at their own pace.

Quality Check *(up to 15 minutes)*

Distribute photocopies of the "Quality Check" handout (p. 16), Bibles, and pens. Have preteens form pairs. Allow students a few minutes to read the Scripture passages and answer the questions on the first part of the handout. Then ask pairs to share responses while a volunteer lists them on newsprint. Have each pair share one quality and how that quality can help them in their friendships, then ask if other pairs have anything new to add. When all the qualities are listed, **ask:**

• Which of these qualities are the most important to you?

• Which of these qualities are the most difficult to show in your friendships?

Direct pairs' attention to the Friendship Situations on the handout. Allow students a few minutes to rate themselves on how they'd react to these situations. When kids have finished, have partners tell each other about one real-life situation where a friend responded to them in a way that showed these qualities.

Say: We've looked at some Scriptures that show us how ➤God can help us develop good friendships. We all have some qualities that help us have good friendships. But there are also ways we can improve and become more like the kind of friends God wants us to be. Let's look into those now.

◄ *The Point*

Life Application

Friendship Improvement *(up to 10 minutes)*

Say: Think about the different biblical qualities of a good friend that we talked about today. Also, think about how you rated yourself on the handout. Based on

all these things, pick one friendship quality you'd like to improve on this week.

Distribute art supplies such as clay, paints, markers, construction paper, drawing paper, and poster board. Have preteens each create a symbol of the friendship quality they need to work on. For example, a student might sculpt or draw a pair of lips to symbolize the need to say positive things to his or her friends. Allow a few minutes for students to create their symbols. **Say: The symbol you've created took some thought and work. In the same way, friendships take work. Even though it may sometimes be challenging for us to do,**

The Point ➤ ➤**God helps us develop good friendships.** Encourage kids to place their symbols in their rooms as a reminder to work at developing that friendship quality.

Wrap-Up Option 1

Friendship Collage *(up to 10 minutes)*

Set out a few stacks of old magazines and several rolls of tape. Form groups of up to five. Provide a sheet of newsprint for each group.

Say: One quality good friends have is that they can work together to accomplish a task. Each group will have four minutes to go through these magazines to find all the words and pictures that show good friendships. Create a collage on your newsprint.

Allow groups four minutes to create their collages. Then have volunteers from each group briefly explain different elements on their group's collage. **Ask:**

• **Is there anything about good friends that you didn't include on your collage? If so, what?**

• **In what ways are the collages like us as we act as friends?**

Say: Let's close by praying in your groups.

Ask groups to gather in a circle. Have one person begin the prayer by praying for the person on the right, praying something like this: Dear God, thank you for [person on right]. Please help [person] be a better friend. Amen.

Wrap-Up Option 2

Friendsong *(up to 10 minutes)*

Before the study, obtain a copy on CD of a current popular song about friendship. Be sure to check the content for appropriateness.

Form a circle and play the song for kids. Have them sing along.

After the song, **ask:**

- **How true is this song to real life?**

- **Is it possible to build friendships with the qualities this song describes? Why or why not?**

Say: Songs may or may not offer a true picture of the friendships we want. But we also know that ➤**God can help us develop good friendships. Let's pray together and ask God to help us be friends that will please him.**

◄ *The Point*

Close with a prayer.

Extra-Time Tips

Friend Art—Use the art supplies from the "Friendship Improvement" activity. Have students form artistic expressions of the friends they have in your preteen group. Kids could create symbols of the friendship qualities they see in one another.

Being a Friend—Have preteens form partners with kids they don't know very well. Give partners a few minutes to tell some things about themselves. Then have partners each share what they learned about their new friend. Encourage partners to extend their newfound friendships outside the preteen meeting.

THE FRIENDSHIP SHOW

Cast: Announcer, Host, Jonathan, King Saul, David, Audience Members 1 to 4

Announcer: Welcome to *The Friendship Show*, the show where audience members get to interview famous friends. And we've got a great story of friendship today. Here's your host—Friendly Frank(ie)! *(Enthusiastic applause)*

Host: Thank you, thank you. Well, we've got quite a story from the Bible today. Some people call it a scandal. Some people don't know what to think. But whatever *you* think, I think it's a hot topic for discussion. Today's topic: "When a Father Really Doesn't Like His Son's Best Friend." Let's welcome our guests now—King Saul, Jonathan, and David! *(Enthusiastic applause)*

Host: OK, guys, now why do you think your relationship has become so intense?

David: I think it's my fault.

Saul: You said that right!

Host: We have an audience member ready to follow up on my original question.

Audience Member 1: Saul, your highness, why do you have such hard feelings toward David?

Saul: I could write a book about it! Let's just put it this way. I go and fight wars and everyone thinks David is the hero. I try to organize a government and everyone wants David to lead them. I try and raise a son *(glares at Jonathan)* and he prefers David to me.

Jonathan: Father, it's not the same.

Audience Member 2: I'd like to ask a question.

Host: OK, go ahead.

Audience Member 2: Yes, another question for his highness, Saul. Sir, it sounds to me like you'd probably be jealous of David whether or not he was your son's friend. Am I right?

Saul: Uh…

Jonathan: Yes, I think he'd be jealous, anyway.

Saul: Wait a minute! Things are bad enough with David without you having him for a friend. I'm trying hard to keep our family in the palace…

David: By killing me?

Jonathan: By killing him? Dad, I couldn't believe my ears when David told me that you wanted him dead. I had to check out his story.

Saul: So you plotted against me!

David: All he did was try to keep me safe, your highness.

Saul: Like I said, he plotted against me!

Audience Member 3: Jonathan, here's my question: Even though you're a prince and would take over your father's throne when he dies, you stuck up for David? I mean, David's the one Samuel anointed to be king after your father!

Saul: Listen to this, son, it makes sense!

Audience Member 3: Do you understand that if David survives, you lose your chance at the throne—maybe forever?

Jonathan: I know. But aren't friends worth more than being a king? *(Enthusiastic audience applause)*

Saul: That's exactly the kind of nonsense I'm talking about. Jonathan, you never talked like this before this—this David came into your life!

Jonathan: Of course not. I never had a friend so great before I met David. It was like our souls were knit together right from the start.

Host: David, do you have anything to say? You're being awfully quiet.

David: Well, it's really hard for me. *(Pauses.)* See, I love and respect the king. *(Audience gasps and murmurs.)*

Audience Member 4: But he's trying to kill you!

David: I know. *(Pauses.)* How do I explain? The King is God's anointed. He's still my king…

Host: That's pretty loyal talk for a guy who has a price on his head.

Jonathan: That's one of the things that make him such a good friend. Dad, you should be ashamed of yourself! How can you hate a guy like this?

Saul: *(Exploding)* You only listen to what you want to hear! I am the KING! If I say someone should die, then he must die! The king has spoken! This friendship can lead to no good. You are my son! I am the king! David must die!

Host: We're just about out of time for today's show. One last question for both David and Jonathan: What makes your friendship special?

Jonathan: Sometimes things just click between two people and a deep friendship develops. Beyond that, David has proven trustworthy and loyal to me. How many other people would stick around after my dad has thrown a spear at them?

Host: Good point! And you, David?

David: Jonathan is nobility, born and raised in a palace. I'm a shepherd and grew up with a bunch of smelly sheep and my harp. But Jonathan never let the difference in our backgrounds make any difference in our friendship. That's a true friend.

Host: I, for one, think it's refreshing to see two young men who are committed to friendship as deeply as you two are. Thank you for being on our show today, and thank you, King Saul, for agreeing to be here as well. *(Applause)*

Announcer: Well, that's all the time we have for *The Friendship Show*. Thanks for being a great audience!

Quality Check

Read the following Scripture passages and answer the questions below:

Proverbs 17:17; Matthew 11:18-19; and John 15:13.

✔ What qualities do these verses say are important in a good friend?

_____
_____
_____
_____

✔ How can these qualities help you have better friendships?

_____
_____
_____
_____

Friendship Situations

How do you think you'd react to these situations? Read each entry and put a check in the column that best describes how closely your reaction would be to what's written. Be honest!

Allie had hurt Meg's feelings badly, but wanted to make things right. She approached Meg at school the day after their fight and said she was sorry. Meg responded, "That's nice, but I'm just not ready to forgive you."

Would you respond like Meg?

I'd respond like Meg:
☐ Most likely _____
☐ Possibly _____
☐ Probably not _____

Ned knew Gregory from church. He didn't mind hanging out with Gregory at church; but at school, Gregory was, well, a lot different from the other kids. One day Gregory caught sight of Ned in the hall and tried to give him the "Jesus Jab" handshake they'd made up at church. Ned ignored him and walked on. Would you have done the same?

I'd respond like Ned:
☐ Most likely _____
☐ Possibly _____
☐ Probably not _____

Sarah and Kyle had grown up next door to each other, but they'd gone in different directions as they grew older. The night Sarah's dad died, Kyle sat up with her and her family even though it meant he'd miss the team bus to the basketball final. Would you make the same choice?

I'd respond like Kyle:
☐ Most likely _____
☐ Possibly _____
☐ Probably not _____

When Friends Disagree

The Point: ➤God can help us handle conflict positively.

Preteens may have grown up in families where conflict was handled in one of two extremes: either avoided at all costs or escalating to all-out battles—or anywhere in between. Conflict has often been labeled negatively, but it is a part of everyone's life. Even Jesus faced conflict, and he showed us how to respond in God-honoring ways.

When conflict occurs in a climate of respect, growth can occur in preteens' lives. Use this study to help students discover positive ways of handling the inevitable conflict they will face.

Scripture Source

Proverbs 25:12; 27:6

These proverbs talk about the importance of being honest with words—even if the words sting. This proverb was written by a man who most likely knew what it meant to receive empty flattery. As king, Solomon depended on those close to him to be honest with him. He wanted them to tell him the truth about himself and his leadership—even if their words might be painful.

Matthew 5:23-24

Jesus teaches about the importance of resolving conflicts with others before we come before God in worship.

Matthew 18:15-20

Jesus gives instructions for resolving conflicts when someone has sinned against us. He taught that dealing directly with conflict is the best way to handle it. He tells us to go immediately to someone if we feel we've been wronged by that person. Instead of publicizing the wrong, Jesus offers steps to heal the relationship as quietly as possible.

The Study at a Glance

Section	Minutes	What Students Will Do	Supplies
Warm-Up Option 1	up to 10	**Disagree to Disagree**—Experience disagreement with a partner.	Photocopies of instruction box (see below)
Warm-Up Option 2	up to 5	**Decorate a Disagreement**—Write and illustrate words that describe feelings when they disagree.	Paper, pencils, markers
Bible Connection	up to 15	**Learning From Conflict**—Create role-plays of conflicts between friends then apply Jesus' teachings in Matthew 5 and 18 to the role-plays.	Bibles, "Help With Conflict" hand-outs (p. 24), pens
	up to 15	**Hurtful or Helpful Words?**—Discuss personal examples of conflict in friendship and explore Proverbs 25:12 and 27:6.	Bibles, index cards, pens
Life Application	up to 10	**Agree to Disagree**—Analyze their own tendencies when facing conflicts in a friendship.	"Agree to Disagree?" handouts (p. 25), pens
Wrap-Up Option 1	up to 10	**Decorate a Disagreement Revisited**—Illustrate words that describe feelings when they know conflict will improve a friendship.	Paper, pencils, markers
Wrap-Up Option 2	up to 5	**Dear Friends…**—Write a letter to a friend that describes how they'll handle conflict in their friendship.	Paper, pens

Before the Study

Set out Bibles, paper, pens, pencils, newsprint, markers, and tape. Make one photocopy of the "Help With Conflict" handout (p. 24) and the "Agree to Disagree" handout (p. 25) for each preteen.

The Study

Warm-Up Option 1

Disagree to Disagree *(up to 10 minutes)*

Have preteens form pairs and give each person a photocopy of the box in the margin. Instruct kids to quietly read their slips without showing them to anyone else.

Say: Each of you has been given instructions. I'm going to read a set of quick directions. You'll have only thirty seconds to decide how you'll respond to each task I give you. Ready?

Read through this series of quick directions, pausing for thirty seconds after each task. **Say: You're getting a new animal. First, decide what kind of animal you're getting. (Pause.) Second, decide what to name it. (Pause.) Third, work** up a schedule of who feeds and gives any other care to the animal. (Pause.) Fourth, decide where the animal will sleep. (Pause.)

After thirty seconds, **ask:**

• **How did you feel when your partner disagreed with all your ideas?**

• **How was this feeling similar to what happens between friends sometimes?**

Say: This activity was designed to force you to disagree with your partner. And it was a pretty silly thing to disagree over.

Ask:

• **What are some more serious disagreements you have with others?**

Say: We all face conflict in some form or another. Sometimes it's over simple things, while other times it's over significant matters. Today we're going to explore what happens when friends disagree. And we'll discover how ➤God can help us handle conflict positively.

◀ *The Point*

Warm-Up Option 2

Decorate a Disagreement *(up to 5 minutes)*

Provide paper, pencils, and markers to students. Instruct students to write down one word that describes how they feel when they disagree with a friend. Then have them decorate the word to make it "look like" the feeling the word represents. For example, if the word is *hurt*, they could draw tears coming out of the word. Give a minute or two for preteens to work. Then allow a few volunteers to share their words and pictures. **Ask:**

• **Were the words and pictures you created negative or positive? Why?**

Say: When we disagree with our friends, it's usually not a pleasant experience. Yet we all face conflict in our lives. And because it's an unpleasant situation, we may not handle it well. Today we're going to explore what happens when friends disagree. And we'll discover how ➤God can help us handle conflict positively.

◀ *The Point*

Bible Connection

Learning From Conflict *(up to 15 minutes)*

Form groups of up to four. Provide Bibles, pens, and a copy of the "Help With Conflict" handout (p. 24) to group members. **Say: On your handouts are two Bible passages that will help us learn from the conflict we face. In your** groups, read the Bible passages listed on your handout, and discuss the questions on the top half of the handout.

Allow groups a few minutes to complete the top half of their handouts. Then **say: In your groups, decide on a situation—either real or one your group makes up—and create a role-play of that situation. The situation needs to involve conflict between friends. First you'll create the role-play that shows the conflict. Then you'll apply the biblical principles you learned from Jesus' teaching and complete the role-play using those principles. The bottom half of your handout has instructions to guide you.**

Allow groups about five minutes to create their role-plays. Then have groups present them to the class. After the role-plays, have groups discuss these questions in their groups. **Ask:**

- **How would you sum up Jesus' advice in Matthew 5:23-24?**
- **Why do you think it's so important to work quickly to resolve conflicts with your friends?**
- **Why do you suppose Jesus taught in Matthew 18:15-20 to first go directly to someone with whom you have a problem?**
- **What do you believe is the toughest thing about resolving conflicts with friends?**

Say: Whenever we have a conflict, it's easy to want to fight or withdraw from the person we're arguing with. But Jesus teaches us that nobody wins when we don't try to resolve our conflicts with others. Jesus' teachings show us how ➤God can help us handle conflict positively.

Now, let's look at another situation that can happen between friends.

FYI

Whenever groups discuss a list of questions, write the questions on newsprint, and tape the newsprint to the wall so groups can discuss the questions at their own pace.

The Point ➤

Hurtful or Helpful Words? *(up to 15 minutes)*

Provide index cards and pens to preteens. **Say: Think about a time you had a conflict with a friend. On your index card, write a few sentences about what happened. But don't reveal how it turned out yet.**

Give students a few minutes to complete their cards. Then have students form pairs and number off one and two in their pairs. **Say: Number ones, tell your partner what you wrote on your card—your job is to listen to what your partner has to say about it. Number twos, your job is to respond to your partner. Tell him or her if you think he or she was in the right or wrong with the conflict.**

Remember, number ones, you must listen to what your partner has to say to you, whether or not you like what you're hearing. We'll switch roles, so you'll both have the opportunity to give advice.

Allow a few minutes for students to work. After twos have responded to their partners, have them read their conflict situations and allow number ones to respond. Then **ask:**

- **What was it like giving advice to your partner?**
- **Do you think friends should give this kind of advice? Why or why not?**

Provide a Bible and ask a volunteer to read Proverbs 25:12 and 27:6 aloud to the group. **Ask:**

- **Why do you think a person's rebuke or correction is a good thing?**
- **What do you think the phrase "Wounds from a friend can be trusted" means?**
- **After hearing these verses, do you feel differently about the activity with your partner? Explain.**

Say: Conflict can come from misinformation or misunderstanding between people. Or it can be caused by the failure or sin of one person. These proverbs show us how ➤God can help us handle conflict positively. Now let's see how we can do this in situations we might face.

◀ *The Point*

Life Application

Agree to Disagree *(up to 10 minutes)*

Distribute photocopies of the "Agree to Disagree?" handouts (p. 25) and pens. Give preteens a few minutes to complete the handouts. Then have students form pairs and share their responses with each other. **Ask:**

- **In one word, how would you describe your feelings when you disagree with a friend?**
- **How would you like your friends to act toward you when they disagree with you?**
- **Think of the last time you disagreed with a friend. How could you have changed the way you acted to make things go more smoothly?**

Say: Conflicts are actually good for a friendship—they serve to bring people closer together. Let's commit together this week to take the disagreements that might come up and allow them to make us better friends.

Have kids pray silently, committing to God that they'll work at resolving their conflicts with friends this week.

Wrap-Up Option 1

Decorate a Disagreement Revisited *(up to 10 minutes)*

Use this option if you used Warm-Up Option 2. Provide paper, pencils and markers to students. Instruct students to write on their papers one word that describes how they feel when they disagree with a friend, but believe their friendship will grow stronger *because* of the conflict. Then have them decorate the word to make it "look like" the feeling the word represents. For example, if the word is *hope*, they could draw a sunrise around the word. Give a minute or two for preteens to work. Then allow a few volunteers to share their words and pictures. Have students retrieve their drawings from the Warm-Up activity. **Ask:**

• **How are the words and pictures you *just* created different from those in the opening activity?**

• **How do you think you'll handle conflicts with your friends now?**

The Point ➤   **Say:** We've discovered how ➤God can help us handle conflict positively. Let's ask him to help us do that in the days ahead.

Close with prayer, asking for God's help in dealing with conflicts in a positive way.

Wrap-Up Option 2

Dear Friends... *(up to 5 minutes)*

Give each student a sheet of paper and a pen. Have each person write a letter to a real friend that completes these thoughts:

Dear _____,

When we have a disagreement, I will try not to _____. But I will try to _____.

Have each student sign his or her letter. Lead preteens in a prayer of commitment to try to be the kind of friends they wrote about in their letters. Encourage them to apply God's ways of resolving problems this week.

Extra-Time Tips

Face to Face—Form two groups. Have the groups face each other. Have one group come up with a conflict between friends, and then have the other group come up with a solution for how to handle that conflict. Then reverse roles.

Disagreement Cheers—As a class or in smaller groups, have kids create cheers that talk about how people can disagree and still be friends. Have class members perform their cheers and then give themselves a round of applause.

Help With Conflict

Jesus' Teachings

Jesus taught on the importance of working through conflict.
Read the passages listed below and answer the questions:

Read Matthew 5:23-24.

• How would you sum up Jesus' advice in this passage?

_____
_____
_____
_____

• How can you apply these words to a situation where you're facing conflict with a friend?

_____
_____
_____
_____

Read Matthew 18:15-20.

• How would you sum up Jesus' advice in this passage?

_____
_____
_____
_____

• How can you apply these words to a situation where you're facing conflict with a friend?

_____
_____
_____
_____

A Conflict Situation

• First summarize the conflict situation your group will role-play:

_____
_____
_____
_____

• Next, apply the principles Jesus taught to your conflict situation and summarize it here:

_____
_____
_____
_____

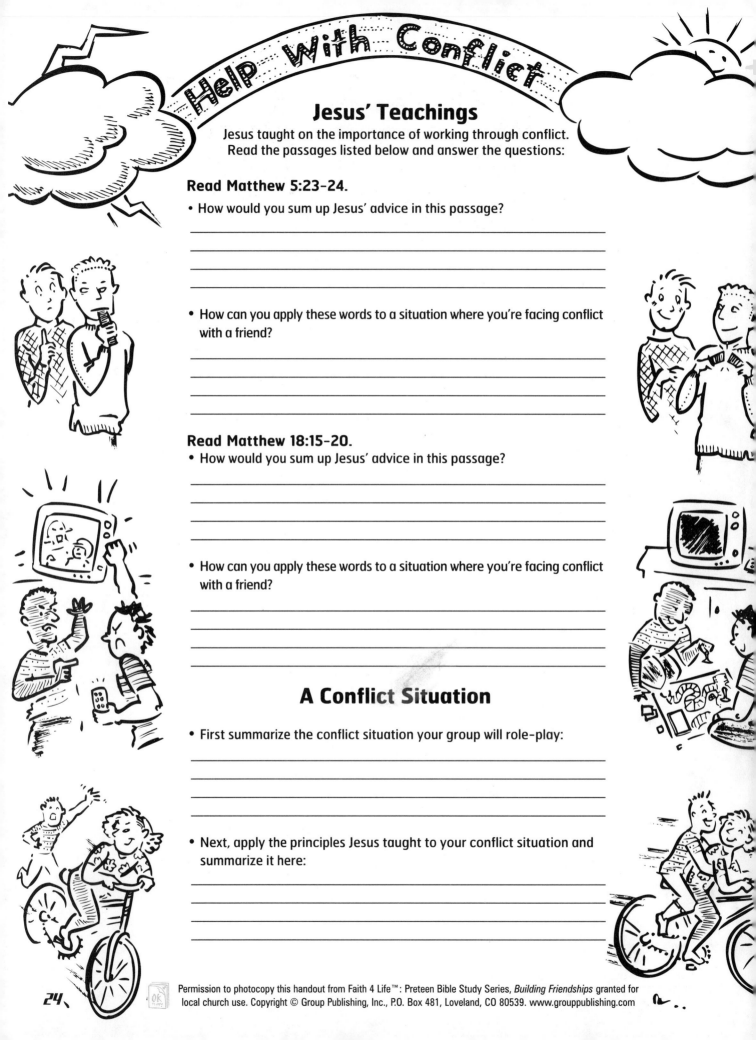

Agree to Disagree?

Read the following situations. Rate the situations on a scale of 1 to 5 (see below),
based on the amount of influence you'd try to exert to get your friend to change his or her behavior.

1	*2*	*3*	*4*	*5*
No influence	**Not much influence**	**Some influence**	**Strong influence**	**Major influence**

1. Your friend wants to go to a party where you know there will be drinking and drugs.

   1   2   3   4   5

2. Your friend meets you before school and shows you a tattoo of a known gang.

   1   2   3   4   5

3. You notice your friend reading information from a group that you think is a cult.

   1   2   3   4   5

4. Your friend is involved in spreading a false rumor about someone whom nobody in school really likes.

   1   2   3   4   5

5. You notice that every day after lunch your friend goes to the bathroom to throw up.

   1   2   3   4   5

6. You happen to be around when your friend steals money from his or her parents.

   1   2   3   4   5

Between Guys and Girls

The Point: ➤ God can help us develop friendships with the opposite sex.

Preteens are caught somewhere between childhood and adulthood. And they often don't know how they're supposed to act toward the opposite sex. These students need to know that God understands their struggle. And he gives insight on how to relate to the opposite sex. Use this study to help preteens develop healthy friendships with the opposite sex.

Scripture Source

Luke 2:41-52

When he was twelve years old, Jesus attended his first Passover feast. When his parents left, Jesus stayed behind without their knowledge to listen to the religious leaders. When his parents came back for him, Jesus obeyed them.

Galatians 3:28

Paul talks about the equality of people in Christ—neither nationality, social standing, nor gender matters in the kingdom of God.

1 Corinthians 13:11-12

Paul encourages Christians to grow in spiritual maturity.

Hebrews 4:14-15

Hebrews explains how Jesus is our High Priest and is personally familiar with the temptations humankind endures—yet he remained sinless.

2 Peter 1:3-11

Peter outlines steps to maturity in Christ. He teaches that a Christian validates his or her call from God by growing toward maturity in Christian qualities. He lists several qualities to be added, one on top of the other, if Christians are to grow in their faith.

The Study at a Glance

Section	Minutes	What Students Will Do	Supplies
Warm-Up Option 1	up to 10	**Quick Draw**—Draw boys' and girls' childhood toys and discuss them.	Newsprint, markers, index cards, pens
Warm-Up Option 2	up to 10	**Tricycle Slalom**—Negotiate a relay course on tricycles.	Plastic cups, 2 tricycles
Bible Connection	up to 15	**Growth Goals**—Examine biblical characteristics of growth and list ways God can help them grow and relate to the opposite sex.	Bibles, "God, Growth, and Me" handouts (p. 35), pens
	up to 15	**Towers of Growth**—Build towers out of boxes that have traits from 2 Peter 1 written on them.	Bibles, 8 shoe boxes, newsprint, tape, markers, paper, pens
Life Application	up to 10	**Super Shield**—Create coats of arms describing their lives.	"My Shield" handouts (p. 36), pens, thin-tipped markers
Wrap-Up Option 1	up to 10	**Growing Pins**—Use a childhood game to learn about trusting God.	Bible, newsprint, marker, paper strips, pencils, blindfolds
Wrap-Up Option 2	up to 5	**Away With Childish Things**—Choose childish characteristics they'll get rid of.	Bible, paper, pens, trash bag

Before the Study

Set out Bibles, paper, pens, newsprint, markers, tape, and thin-tipped markers. Make one photocopy of the "God, Growth, and Me" handout (p. 35) and the "My Shield" handout (p. 36) for each preteen. Also write each toy on a separate index card from the Guys' Toys and Girls' Toys lists on page 29. If using Wrap-Up Option 1, make an enlarged copy of the stick-figure donkey (p. 33) on a sheet of newsprint.

The Study

Warm-Up Option 1

Quick Draw (up to 10 minutes)

Before kids arrive, stack the index cards prepared earlier into a boys' toy stack and a girls' toy stack. When students arrive, gather guys into one group and girls into another. **Say: Today we're going to talk about guys, girls, friendships, and God. To start, we're going to play a game about toys we played with when we were little kids.**

Give each group newsprint and a marker. Tell groups they'll each guess common childhood toys as they're drawn by team members. Have the girls use the

"Guys' Toys" cards, and have the guys use the "Girls' Toys" cards.

Have groups each choose one volunteer to turn over the top card in the stack and draw the toy on their group's newsprint. The volunteer may not speak or write any words on the newsprint. When a group guesses the toy correctly, have another group member draw the next toy.

After both groups have guessed all the cards, gather preteens together. **Ask:**

• **How easy was it to guess toys that members of the opposite sex played with?**

• **Do you agree with the list for the guy toys and the list for the girl toys? Why or why not?**

• **Do guys and girls play differently? Explain.**

• **Why do you think guys are drawn to some toys and girls are drawn to others? Explain.**

Say: This game helped you see both the differences and the similarities between guys and girls when you were children. Some toys you both played with, while others are mostly for one sex or the other. Now, as preteens, your relationships with the opposite sex are changing. Today we're going to look at guy/girl friendships and how ➤God can help us develop friendships with the opposite sex.

Warm-Up Option 2

Tricycle Slalom *(up to 10 minutes)*

This activity will require a larger area, such as a gym floor or empty parking lot. Set up a simple slalom course using plastic cups to indicate the flags on the course (see illustration).

When students arrive, have guys form one group and girls another. It's OK if groups are uneven. The number of people in the larger group determines the number of relay laps for the challenge. Gather kids in front of the slalom course you set up. **Say: Today we're going to talk about guys, girls, friendships, and God. To start, we're going to have a little challenge—welcome to the Tricycle Slalom! Each person will ride the tricycle up and back through the slalom course, weaving in and out of the cones. In your group, line up alphabetically according to the first letters of your middle names. If your team has fewer people than the other team, you'll need to have some people go to the end of the line after their turn and ride another slalom leg.**

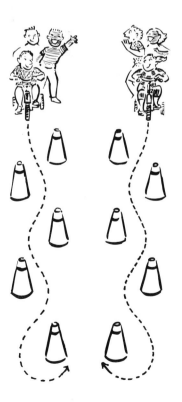

Toy List

Guys' Toys

• *chemistry set*

• *skateboard*

• *electric train*

• *toy cars*

• *building blocks*

• *coloring books*

• *video games*

Girls' Toys

• *playhouse*

• *dolls*

• *stuffed animals*

• *mother's clothes*

• *building blocks*

• *coloring books*

• *video games*

The Point ➤

Have the first person in each line sit on the tricycle (or stand behind it with one foot on the base, depending on the size of the tricycle). On "go," have them pedal up and down the course. Once they reach the starting point, have the next person in line take his or her turn riding the course.

When everyone has completed the course, gather students together. **Ask:**

• **Do you think you would have done better if you had groups of both guys and girls? Explain.**

• **How is this slalom like the way guys and girls relate in everyday situations?**

• **Why do guys and girls like to do things in same-sex groups?**

Say: **As you've grown out of childhood, you've probably found most of your friends are of the same sex. It's easy to associate with only guys if you're a guy or only girls if you're a girl. But as you head into adulthood, you're going to want more friends of the opposite sex. Today we're going to look at guy/girl friendships and how** ➤**God can help us develop friendships with the opposite sex.**

Bible Connection

Growth Goals *(up to 15 minutes)*

Give a volunteer a Bible and ask him or her to read Galatians 3:28 aloud. **Ask:**

• **What does this verse say to you about men and women from a spiritual perspective?**

Say: **Paul makes it clear in this verse that men and women are spiritually equal in Christ's eyes. With that truth as a starting point, we can look at what the Bible says about maturity.**

Have students form same-gender groups of up to four. Provide Bibles and give each student a photocopy of the "God, Growth, and Me" handout (p. 35) and a pen. Ask for a few volunteers to read Luke 2:41-52 aloud to the class. **Say:** **Jesus was about your age when he taught the Jewish leaders in the Temple. Ask:**

• **What can you learn about Jesus' growth from these verses?**

Say: **Jesus grew intellectually, physically, spiritually, and socially. And you are all maturing in these areas—in some areas more than in others.**

Have students complete their handouts in their groups. Once they've done this, have them form mixed-gender groups as equally as possible. Then, based on how preteens filled out the handout, have each of them share one way to show respect to the opposite sex. After all group members have shared within their groups, **ask:**

• **How does it feel to know God is with you during your maturing process?**

• **What are some of the struggles preteens face with growing up and relating to one another?**

• **Do you think Jesus struggled with growing up? Explain.**

Ask a volunteer to read Hebrews 4:14-15 aloud to the class.

Say: **This verse says Jesus faced all the temptations we face. And it would be safe to say the temptations and struggles of growing up and learning how to relate to the opposite sex would be included in that list. This activity has helped us see how ➤God can help us develop friendships with the opposite sex. Now let's work together on some common goals.**

◀ *The Point*

Towers of Growth *(up to 15 minutes)*

Have preteens form eight groups, and give each group a Bible, a shoe box, a sheet of newsprint, scissors, tape, paper, pens, and markers. (A group can consist of one person.) If you have fewer than eight people, form four groups and give each group two boxes. Have groups cover the shoe boxes with newsprint, using scissors and tape. Ask a volunteer to read 2 Peter 1:3-4 aloud to the class. **Ask:**

• **How would you summarize these verses in your own words?**

• **How can you claim the promises mentioned in these verses?**

Assign each group one of the growth characteristics from 2 Peter 3:5b-7: faith, goodness, knowledge, self-control, perseverance, godliness, brotherly kindness, and love. Have groups each come up with a definition of their quality and write it on their shoe-box block. Then have group members write a few ways they might demonstrate that quality, especially as it concerns the opposite sex. For example, they might write *perseverance*—not reacting unkindly to a person who rejects them."

When groups have finished, have kids stack the blocks in the center of the room in the order they appear in the passage. Then have each group explain its block. **Ask:**

• **How is building this tower like "building" ourselves as we grow and mature?**

• **How is this tower like the qualities it represents?**

• **Are there certain qualities girls or guys develop faster than the opposite sex? Explain.**

FYI

Whenever groups discuss a list of questions, write the questions on newsprint, and tape the newsprint to the wall so groups can discuss the questions at their own pace.

Have girls stack the blocks according to the importance they feel each item has—with the item they think is the most important on top. Have the girls tell why they stacked the blocks in that order. Then have guys do the same. Discuss similarities guys and girls had in the order of items in their towers.

The Point ➤ **Say: All the characteristics written on these blocks work together to make us more like Christ. Striving to grow in these areas pleases God and helps you relate better to the opposite sex. ➤God can help us develop friendships with the opposite sex. Now let's see how these characteristics might already be evident in your lives.**

Life Application

Super Shield *(up to 10 minutes)*

Say: The positive qualities you have now and the efforts you make to grow them will make a difference in how you relate to the opposite sex.

Have preteens spread out so none of them are close together. Give each student a "My Shield" handout (p. 36). Provide pens and thin-tipped markers. **Say: Your handout shows a picture of a shield. In older cultures, families decorated a shield of armor with characteristics of their family or ancestors. It was called a coat of arms and was an important source of pride for the family. It gave them identity and was a visual representation of what the family was. Now you're going to make a personal coat of arms that describes you.**

Have students each create a personal coat of arms by drawing pictures in each section. When they've finished, have them form pairs or trios. As much as possible, have a guy and girl be partners. Have partners briefly share their completed handouts.

Say: As we can see from these shields, both guys and girls have God-given strengths that will help them grow and mature into adulthood. By recognizing one another's strengths, we can learn to respect one another for who we are, not for what sex we happen to be.

Have kids each silently commit to looking for positive qualities in others, regardless of their gender.

Wrap-Up Option 1

Growing Pins *(up to 10 minutes)*

Say: As we grow up, we grow out of certain childhood activities. But we can still learn from the games we played as kids. Today we're going to end the study with a variation on a familiar party game, Pin the Tail on the Donkey.

Form no fewer than three groups. Have each team pick a representative to play Pin the Tail on the Donkey. Copy the stick-figure donkey from the margin onto a sheet of newsprint. Give each representative a paper strip with tape at one end, and have them each write their name on it. Have teams act as cheering sections for their representatives, but don't allow them to give directions.

Blindfold each representative. One at a time, spin the representatives and have them stick their tails as close to the target as possible. Don't allow representatives to remove their blindfolds until the game is over. Silently remove the last player's blindfold just before he or she is spun. Be sure kids don't let the other representatives know what's happened. After the last representative places the tail correctly on the donkey, have representatives remove their blindfolds. **Ask** the representatives:

• **What did you think about this game?**

Explain what you did with the last player. Then **ask:**

• **How much easier is it to pin the tail on the donkey when you don't have a blindfold?**

• **What can we do to "take off the blindfolds" as we deal with members of the opposite sex?**

Say: Even if you feel awkward, clumsy, or self-conscious around girls or guys, you can trust God because he knows what you're going through.

Read Luke 2:52 aloud. Close with a prayer thanking God for the growth of your preteens. Ask for God's help for girls and guys to grow and learn how to relate to one another.

Wrap-Up Option 2

Away With Childish Things *(up to 5 minutes)*

Say: As we grow up and learn to relate to the opposite sex, we need to put away childish attitudes and actions. When we stop gossiping about one another or calling one another names, we can spend quality time getting to know one another as people—no matter what sex we are.

Ask a volunteer to read 1 Corinthians 13:11-12 aloud. Give preteens each a sheet of paper and a pen, and have them each write one childish characteristic they'll get rid of. For example, kids might write "temper tantrums" or "fighting." When students have finished, go around the circle holding out a trash bag. As you walk by, have each person read aloud his or her childish trait, crumple the paper, and throw it in the bag.

Form a circle and close in prayer. Thank God for positive childlike qualities and the preteens' ability to enjoy those characteristics in one another as they relate to the opposite sex.

Extra-Time Tips

Are They for Real?—Form groups of no more than five. Give each group paper and a pen. Have group members list movies or TV shows about older teenagers, listing the dominant qualities of the teenage characters and then dividing the characters according to whether group members think the characters are "real" or "Hollywood." Have groups share their lists with the class. Then have kids tell which older teenage qualities they want to develop.

Girls and Guys—Write the words *girls* and *guys* vertically down the middle of a sheet of newsprint or a chalkboard. Have kids work together to brainstorm words or phrases illustrating positive aspects of both girls and guys, using the letters to form an acrostic. For example:

Good listeners   **G**enerous

Interested in relationships   **U**nderstanding

Ready to help   **Y**oung at heart

Likable   **S**mart

Super friends

God, Growth & Me

How can God help you grow and learn how to relate to the opposite sex? Under each of the four categories, write some goals you have and how God can help you with those goals. You won't have as much control over your physical goals, but you could write ways you need God to help you through the physical changes.

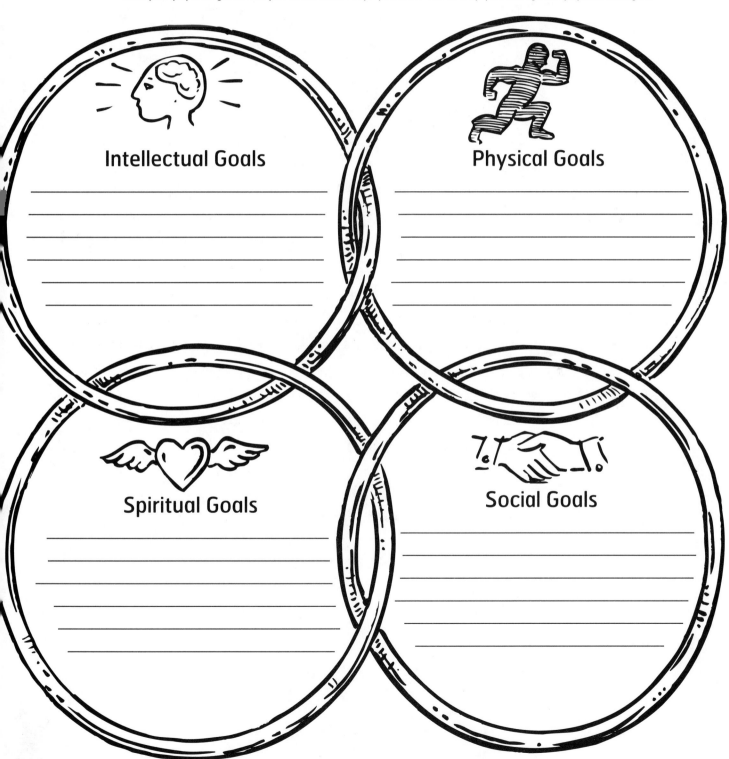

Intellectual Goals

Physical Goals

Spiritual Goals

Social Goals

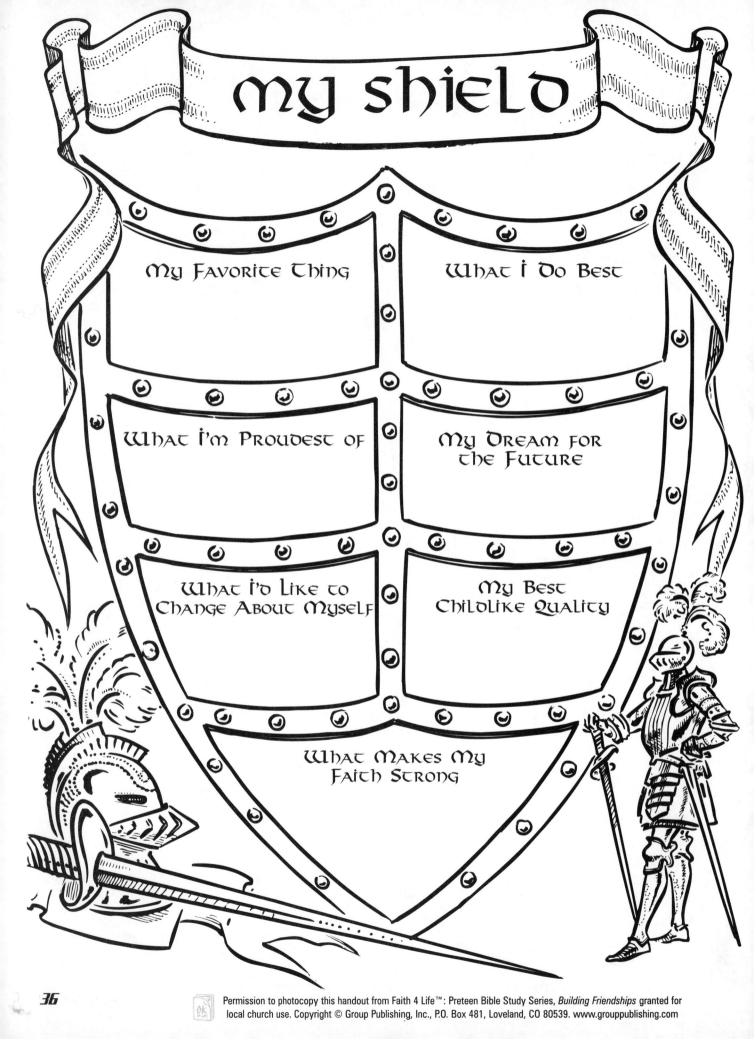

my shield

My Favorite Thing

What I Do Best

What I'm Proudest of

My Dream for the Future

What I'd Like to Change About Myself

My Best Childlike Quality

What Makes My Faith Strong

More Than a Friend

The Point: ➤ Jesus can be our perfect friend.

For preteens, friendships are becoming an important priority. And the importance of friendships only grows as kids mature. As they face the struggles of building friendships, they may get discouraged with their relationships. But you can encourage them to build a relationship with the one friend who will never let them down—Jesus. Use this study to help preteens develop and nurture a special relationship that goes beyond friendship—one that will last through eternity!

Scripture Source

John 6:35; 8:12; 10:14-15; 11:25-26; 14:6

John records the "I am" statements Jesus makes about himself. Jesus used several metaphors to designate himself and his relationship with the Father. Among these, Jesus describes himself as the bread of life, the light of the world, the good shepherd, the resurrection and the life, and the way, the truth, and the life.

John 15:13-15

Jesus defines the greatest love as laying down one's life for friends. He tells his disciples that he looks at them as friends, not servants. Jesus describes his friends as those who do what he commands.

The Study at a Glance

Section	Minutes	What Students Will Do	Supplies
Warm-Up Option 1	up to 10	**A Perfect Friend?**—List qualities of the ideal friend.	Newsprint, markers
Warm-Up Option 2	up to 10	**Cliffhangers**—Brainstorm cliffhangers and discuss how a perfect friend would solve them.	Index cards, pens
Bible Connection	up to 15	**A Special Friend**—Form friendships and interview each other, then explore Jesus' "I am" statements in the Gospel of John.	Bibles, colored sheets of paper, pens, "Friendship Pieces" handout (p. 43), scissors
	up to 15	**Picture of a Friend**—Create murals based on Jesus' teaching in John 15:13-15.	Bibles, tape, newsprint, markers
Life Application	up to 10	**My Perfect Friend**—Examine how Jesus is Lord and Savior and evaluate their relationship with him.	Bibles, "Friendship Pieces" handout pieces (used previously)
Wrap-Up Option 1	up to 10	**Picture-Perfect Friend**—Draw ways they can be more committed to Jesus.	Murals from the "Picture of a Friend" activity, markers
Wrap-Up Option 2	up to 10	**Cliffhangers Revisited**—Discuss cliffhangers and how Jesus would or wouldn't resolve them.	Index cards from the "Cliffhangers" activity

Before the Study

Set out Bibles, paper, pens, newsprint, markers, paper in a variety of colors, and tape. Make one photocopy of the "Friendship Pieces" handout (p. 43) and cut apart the five pieces from the handout.

The Study

Warm-Up Option 1

A Perfect Friend? *(up to 10 minutes)*

Have preteens list on newsprint qualities of the ideal friend. No quality is too wild, even if they think it's impossible for someone to fulfill.

After students have had a few minutes to develop the list, review it with them. Then **ask:**

• **Do you really know anyone who might fulfill all these positive qualities? Explain.**

• **If you had that sort of friend, what would you want him or her to do for you as a friend?**

- **Do you think this kind of person would ever fail you as a friend?**

Say: It's nearly impossible to think of any person totally fulfilling the role of a perfect friend. We've been looking at friendships these past few studies, and we've discovered ways to be a better friend. But no matter how much we try, we all fall short in our friendships. Today we're going to look at a relationship that will never fail us and explore how ▶Jesus can be our perfect friend.

◀ *The Point*

Warm-Up Option 2

Cliffhangers *(up to 10 minutes)*

Have everyone sit in a circle, and distribute index cards and pens. Have preteens each write a "cliffhanger" on their card—this should be a really tough situation (of any type) that looks impossible to get out of. Ask students to each pass their card to the person on their left—who must write on it exactly how a perfect friend might rescue the person or resolve the problem. Students will then pass the cards once more to the left. Have the final recipient of each card read it to the rest of the group.

After one round of Cliffhangers, **ask:**

- **What do you think it would be like to have a perfect friend?**
- **Do you think this kind of person would ever fail you as a friend?**

Say: It's nearly impossible to think of any person who could be called the perfect friend. We've been looking at friendships these past few studies and discovered ways to be a better friend. But no matter how much we try, we all fall short in our friendships. Today we're going to look at a relationship that will never fail us and explore how ▶Jesus can be our perfect friend.

◀ *The Point*

Bible Connection

A Special Friend *(up to 15 minutes)*

For this study, you'll need the five cut-up pieces from the "Friendship Pieces" handout (p. 43) that you copied earlier. You'll also need two sheets of the same color paper for every student in your class. If you have fourteen students, you'll need twenty-eight sheets, two of each color. Randomly mix the colored sheets and place them in a stack.

Say: We're going to form some quick friendships in the next few minutes.

Give each preteen one color sheet and a pen, and explain that they should find another student with the same color sheet.

Say: Now that you've found a new friend, take a few minutes to find out more about him or her. Write down what your partner tells you on your paper. Here are some questions to get you started. **Ask:**

- **What makes you a good friend?**
- **What is something special you've done for a friend?**
- **When did you let down a friend?**

Allow students a few minutes to interview each other. Circulate around and encourage students as needed. After students have recorded their interviews, have them gather together. **Ask:**

- **What did you learn about your partner?**
- **How did it feel to share a time you let down a friend?**
- **Could you call yourself the perfect friend? Explain.**

Say: As you got to know more about your new friend in this activity, you learned some ways he or she could be called a good friend. But you also heard ways that friends let one another down. We've all let our friends down. But wouldn't it be great to know a friend who wouldn't ever let us down?

The Point ➤ Well, ➤Jesus can be our perfect friend. Let's see why.

Form five groups. Give each group a Bible and one piece from the "Friendship Pieces" handout (p. 43). **Say: Each group has a saying Jesus spoke about himself. In your groups, look up the passage and follow the instructions on your piece of paper.**

Allow students a few minutes to complete the instructions. Then ask volunteers to share their groups' responses.

Say: Unlike our earthly friends, Jesus is a perfect friend who won't let us down. Let's look at this further.

Have groups keep the handout pieces for use in the "My Perfect Friend" activity.

Picture of a Friend *(up to 15 minutes)*

Have preteens remain in their groups. Give groups newsprint and markers, and have them gather around tables. Ask a volunteer to read John 15:13-15 aloud. Have groups discuss these questions. **Ask:**

- **What sort of things do you think people who want to be Jesus' friend will do, according to this passage?**
- **How does Jesus show us he is our friend?**

• What is one way you could illustrate this?

Say: Based on your group discussions, create a mural that shows how Jesus is a friend and how you are a friend to him.

Allow students about five minutes to create their drawings. Then have groups display their murals, and allow a few minutes for everyone to look at all the murals.

Ask:

• How did the murals help you see how Jesus is your friend?

• How did the murals show you obeying Jesus?

• In what ways is it hard for you to obey Jesus?

Say: You may not need to obey your friends. But Jesus is a friend who commands our obedience to him. ▶Jesus can be our perfect friend. But he gives us the choice. Let's look at what having a relationship with Jesus means.

◀ *The Point*

Life Application

My Perfect Friend *(up to 10 minutes)*

Have students return to their groups from the previous two activities. Have a volunteer from each group retrieve the group's paper slip (from the "Friendship Pieces" handout). Ask another volunteer from each group to read the Scripture listed on the slip aloud to the class. Then have someone from each group bring the paper up to the front of the room. Give these volunteers a minute to put the paper pieces in the correct order, revealing a picture of a cross in the background. Tape the pieces together and hold up the reassembled handout for everyone to see.

Say: We just heard the "I am" statement of Jesus that you looked at earlier. When we put all these statements together, we can see the picture of a cross. Jesus is the perfect friend because only he could offer forgiveness for our sins. Let's take a minute to think about our faith commitment to Jesus.

Allow a minute for students to reflect on their relationship with Jesus. **Say:** ▶Jesus can be our perfect friend. Jesus laid down his life for us and he asks us to lay down our lives for him.

◀ *The Point*

Wrap-Up Option 1

Picture-Perfect Friend *(up to 10 minutes)*

Have students think of ways they want to commit to Jesus, and have them draw or write those ways on their murals from the "Picture of a Friend" activity.

FYI

Whenever groups discuss a list of questions, write the questions on newsprint, and tape the newsprint to the wall so groups can discuss the questions at their own pace.

The Point ➤

Allow volunteers to share their creative expressions. **Say: You've shown how** ➤**Jesus can be our perfect friend. Let's thank God for giving Jesus for us.**

Close with prayer, thanking God for sending Jesus to be our perfect friend.

Wrap-Up Option 2

Cliffhangers Revisited *(up to 10 minutes)*

Use this option if you used the Warm-Up Option 2 activity. Gather the index cards used in the "Cliffhangers" activity, and pass them out randomly to the class. Have preteens each write a fresh resolution to their cliffhanger, using Jesus as the perfect friend coming to the rescue. Have students explain their cliffhangers to the group. **Ask:**

- **Is Jesus the kind of friend who would help in these situations or not?**
- **What kinds of situations would Jesus help you with?**

Say: Jesus is concerned with helping us in ways we truly need it. That's another reason to thank him for being our perfect friend.

Close with prayer, thanking God for sending Jesus to be our perfect friend.

Extra-Time Tips

Jesus Friend—Have preteens brainstorm situations for which they need the help of a friend. Then have them discuss how Jesus might help in those situations.

Dear Jesus—You could use this idea during the Life Application or Wrap-Up sections. Distribute paper and pens and have preteens write letters to Jesus about their relationship with him.

Friendship Pieces

John 6:35

Write Jesus' statement in your own words.

_____
_____

How does Jesus' statement help you see him as your best friend?

_____
_____
_____

John 8:12

Write Jesus' statement in your own words.

_____
_____

How does Jesus' statement help you see him as your best friend?

_____
_____
_____

John 10:14-15

Write Jesus' statement in your own words.

_____
_____

How does Jesus' statement help you see him as your best friend?

_____
_____
_____

John 11:25-26

Write Jesus' statement in your own words.

_____
_____

How does Jesus' statement help you see him as your best friend?

_____
_____
_____

John 14:6

Write Jesus' statement in your own words.

_____
_____

How does Jesus' statement help you see him as your best friend?

_____
_____

Use this activity to show preteens the importance of friends helping and serving. Hold a Saturday retreat that focuses on serving others as friends.

Before the retreat, secretly get permission from preteens' parents to do the following "Good Samaritan" activity. At the beginning of the retreat, have some preteens read the story of the good Samaritan in Luke 10:25-37. Have students discuss the question: Who is my neighbor? Encourage preteens to see how they can help out their neighbors in need. Then take kids to their homes and have them each pick out three items of quality clothing they could give to the needy.

Have preteens meet with their clothing at a local homeless shelter to offer their gifts of friendship. Have students interact with the people if possible. Then return to the church and discuss the experience.

EVALUATION FOR

Faith 4 Life: Building Friendships

Please help Group Publishing, Inc., continue to provide innovative and useful resources for ministry. Please take a moment to fill out this evaluation and mail or fax it to us. Thanks!

Group Publishing, Inc.
Attention: Product Development
P.O. Box 481
Loveland, CO 80539
Fax: (970) 292-4370

● ● ●

1. As a whole, this book has been (circle one)
not very helpful   *very helpful*
  1   2   3   4   5   6   7   8   9   10

2. The best things about this book:

3. Ways this book could be improved:

4. Things I will change because of this book:

5. Other books I'd like to see Group publish in the future:

6. Would you be interested in field-testing future Group products and giving us your feedback? If so, please fill in the information below:

Name _____

Church Name _____

Denomination _____ Church Size_____

Church Address _____

City_____ State _____ ZIP _____

Church Phone _____

E-mail _____

Look for the Whole Family of Faith 4 LifE™ Bible Studies!

Preteen Books
- Being Responsible
- Building Friendships
- Getting Along With Others
- God in My Life
- Going Through Tough Times
- Handling Conflict
- How to Make Great Choices
- Peer Pressure
- Succeeding in School
- The Bible and Me
- What's a Christian?
- Why God Made Me

Junior High Books
- Becoming a Christian
- Choosing Wisely
- Fighting Temptation
- Finding Your Identity
- Friends
- God's Purpose for Me
- How to Pray
- My Family Life
- My Life as a Christian
- Sharing Jesus
- Understanding the Bible
- Who Is God?

Senior High Books
- Applying God's Word
- Believing in Jesus
- Christian Character
- Family Matters
- Following Jesus
- Is There Life After High School?
- Prayer
- Sexuality
- Sharing Your Faith
- Worshipping 24/7
- Your Christian ID
- Your Relationships

The Youth Bible
The Bible to use with Faith 4 Life.

Visit your local Christian bookstore,
or contact Group Publishing, Inc., at 800-447-1070.
www.grouppublishing.com

"Ultimate" Preteen Necessities

The Ultimate Book of Preteen Devotions

Take the challenge of ministering to preteens to the edge! They're sure to connect with these 75 Bible-based devotions. From setting goals to materialism to dealing with divorce—these topics and many others are included in the 6 big themes found in this ultimate book:

• Faith

• Friends

• Family

• School

• My World

• Special Days

Plus, easy-prep devotional activities use different learning styles—and multiple intelligences—to reach all preteens. Scripture index included.

ISBN 0-7644-2588-9

The Preteen Worker's Encyclopedia of Bible-Teaching Ideas

Make the New Testament come alive to your preteens and help them discover Bible truths in a big way! In this comprehensive collection, you get nearly 200 creative ideas and activities including: object lessons, skits, games, devotions, service projects, creative prayers, affirmations, creative readings, retreats, parties, trips and travel, and music ideas.

Flexible for any group setting, you'll easily find the perfect idea with helpful Scripture and theme indexes.

ISBN 0-7644-2425-4

The Ultimate Book of Preteen Games

They're not children. Not teenagers. What do you do with preteens? Have a blast! Start with these 100 games they'll love! In the process, you'll break down cliques, build relationships, explore relevant Bible truths, give thought-provoking challenges, and have high-energy fun!

ISBN 0-7644-2291-X

Order today from your local Christian bookstore, online at www.grouppublishing.com or write: Group Publishing, P.O. Box 485, Loveland, CO 80539-0485.

Preteen Boredom Busters

Emotion Explosion!: 40 Devotions for Preteen Ministry

Carol Mader

Show young teenagers that God cares about how they feel. These 40 fun devotions based on the Psalms explore the highs and lows of the life of David, and help preteens take their feelings of doubt and sorrow, hope and joy to God.

ISBN 0-7644-2221-9

Group's Best Jr. High Meetings, Vol. 1

An action-packed collection of the best meetings for junior highers! Meetings include easy-to-use plans and guidelines and cover topics like self-esteem, friendships, parents, faith, and how to make good decisions.

ISBN 0-931529-58-1

Move young teenagers even deeper into worship!

Worshipmania: 80 Active Worship Experiences for Young Teenagers

Worshipmania gives you a collection of 80 unique and uplifting worship activities for young teenagers. Includes traditional forms of worship plus new, innovative ideas. Activities are easy to prepare and easy to take part in—even for self-conscious teenagers. Give your kids a vital understanding of worship and bring them face to face with the love and majesty of their Creator. Introduce them to *Worshipmania* today!

ISBN 0-7644-2195-6